Bulletproof Leadership

BY ANGEL OLVERA

Bulletproof Leadership

© Angel Olvera

In accordance with the u.s. copyright act of 1976, the scanning, uploading, and electronic sharing of any part of this book without the permission of the publisher is unlawful piracy and theft of the author's intellectual property. If you would like to use material from the book (other than for review purposes), prior written permission must be obtained by contacting the author at business@angelolvera.com. Thank you for your support of the author's rights.

First Edition: June 2021

ISBN-13: 9780996931465

Published by OmediO in Los Angeles, CA

This book is dedicated to all the circumstances, mentors, friends, family, streets, businesses and everyone who told me I would never succeed.

Table of Contents

Table of Contents 5

Introduction 6

Motivation 18

Communication 40

Positivity 56

Delegation 68

Creativity 78

Trustworthiness 88

Visionary 98

Time Management 108

Influence 120

Decision Making 132

What's Next? 142

About the Author 150

Introduction

WHY

I'm the oldest of the kids in my immediate family. And I think just for that reason, I ended up in leadership roles growing up. Whether it was when we played sports, or with getting the younger kids in line, or for anything else.

I didn't know it at the time because as a kid, I just thought that I was just there to tell people what to do. Part of leadership is telling people what to do… PART of it. Growing up with those roles, it put me in a position to make decisions and to take action first. Of course I didn't know if a decision was right or wrong, or well-thought out, I just did it.

In sports, if I was the oldest player on the field, I was the team captain. In the neighborhood, I could influence my peers just like the older ones could influence me. I figured out pretty quick that leadership is influence. I also figured out that you can use your influence in good and bad ways. I've seen people be influenced by others into doing wrong things, innocent people getting into big time trouble by going to jail or even dying.

After getting kicked out of high school and having a kid at a young age, I started working as a cabinet maker in a shop. I was the youngest apprentice there and I moved up the ranks quickly becoming a journey man. I worked my way up and became the leader of the young apprentices who worked under my lead. I lead them by making sure I showed them the right way to run heavy machinery and how to use certain things efficiently. It was also my job to look out for them because one wrong move and you could lose a finger. I was also over seeing what they were doing. That experience taught me how to lead, influence, AND manage.

When I got into business at the age of 23, I quickly landed in a leadership role way different than working in the shop. This time, I was leading people to become better leaders and entrepreneurs themselves so they can go out and lead their organizations successfully. I was in direct sales so we had to teach people how to work with other people by developing teams in building a sales force.

I made many mistakes in the beginning because being a leader as an entrepreneur is different than being a leader at a job. At a job, you usually lead with fear. People will listen to you because they don't want to lose their job so they do things to play it safe... even if they don't want to. Leading in business with a volunteer army is different because now your leading with influence.

"Why are they following you? Why should anyone want to follow you?" They asked me those questions many years ago. I used to sit back and think about them for a long time to figure out the real reason why. One of my mentors told me, "You have to become the person that you would want to follow." I started reading Fortune 500, Forbes, Success magazines and I started to emulate those executives in the stories. I started to emulate how my mentors would dress, how they would talk, their walk, the whole 9 yards so I can attract better leaders to my organization. "You have to become the person that you would want to follow." It stuck with me.

So the question I have for you is, "Why should anyone want to follow YOU?" In this book, I'm gonna teach you how to become that bulletproof leader that anyone would want to follow, in all aspects of your life: business, sports, family, everything.

FAIL FORWARD

Growing up, I was a really good student and baseball player and my parents had high expectations for me. Then when I started high school, I started going to parties, going out with girls, and hanging out with gangs. According to everyone, it was my downfall when I got kicked out of high school and became a father at 16 years old.

My father looked at me and said "Mijo, I'm getting you a job." He knew the owner of this cabinet shop and that's when I started working there. I started an apprenticeship program where I went to trade school. I had this heavy weight on my shoulders because I let my parents down and made them really young grandparents (I made my mom a grandma when she was in her 30s). When I would be at work sweeping sawdust I would think, "How did I get myself in this situation?"

I felt like a failure. I felt like I let my family down. I had the potential to play baseball in College and here I was sweeping sawdust in a 100 degree heat getting dirty.

So I made a decision that "I'm gonna be the best cabinet maker here" and "I'm gonna be the best apprentice and move up the ranks to show my father appreciation for getting me this job."

Then at 23, I met a guy that was my age living the life I wanted to live. He had a nice house in the Hollywood Hills, drove exotic cars, but the best part was he didn't have a boss. He was able wake up when he wanted, do what he wanted at anytime. Looking back, it was a perfect time to have met this guy because at that time, I did not like my boss and hated that I had to wake up at 5am everyday. I couldn't see myself doing this for the rest of my life.

He invited me to a business presentation. I had NEVER been to any business anything so I was not prepared. I had to borrow a sports coat from my father. The sleeves were a little short, it was baggy in all the wrong places, it looked just like you're thinking it looked... but I had never worn sports coats before so I felt like a boss. I went to the meeting and I met a bunch of business owners that were excited about a new business project. I thought to myself, "I need to be around people like this." It was different than the cabinet shop where everyone was so negative. So I made a decision that night to join them and it changed my life. Everyone is one decision away from changing our lives and that was it for me.

He mentored me and I was able to walk away from my Cabinet Maker job in 6 months. For those 6 months, I was developing as a leader and was already helping others develop themselves. We made a bunch of mistakes in the beginning and it was frustrating, but we kept going.

What I learned in the process is that failure is fertilizer. I read a book called Failing Forward and it changed the way I looked at failure. Remember, I thought I was a failure, that I let my parents down. But when I learned that failure is fertilizer, that if you learn from it, it's a good thing. When we're young, we are taught that failure is bad, like getting an F on your report card. In business and life, failure is good as long as you learn from it. I learned to think of this this way: I'm 5'9, if I fall flat on my face I'll be 5'9 closer to where I want to be. It's about getting back up and keep going.

Baseball is a great example; if you hit the ball 3 out of 10 times, you make millions and are in the hall of fame. But if you hit 2 out of 10 times, just one less, no ones heard of you.

LEADERS GET UP, SHOW UP, AND DON'T QUIT.

GRIT

"Grit is passion and perseverance for very long-term goals." Thats from American psychologist Angela Lee Duckworth, who currently has some important studies into the role grit plays in success. "Grit is having stamina. Grit is sticking with your future, day in, day out, not just for the week, not just for the month, but for years, and working really hard to make that future a reality."

As I read books and went to seminars and went through personal growth, I learned that without even knowing what Grit was, I had it. I'm not going to lie, it was painful and it was uncomfortable. Ever since I can remember, I've always had a NO QUIT attitude. When I got into business, I was gonna finish what I started no matter what and let me tell you, it was tough. I had to grow as a person and then I had to deal with people... which is crazy because sometimes people are crazy. All the things that come along in business and on your way to success; haters, backstabbers, people quit on you or try to bring your business down and some of those people are close to you which is a big blow to the gut.

What kept me going was my why and my no quit attitude, my Grit. Even when I didn't feel like doing things I did them. Late nights, no money, slow success, I still kept going because I had a clear vision of what my life would look like. I see so many proud people reading books, listening to audios, going to seminars about personal development... but their lives stay the same. You have to have Grit and be patient because success doesn't happen overnight, it's a process not an event!

Leaders with Grit are always leading from the front meaning leading by example, not just telling people what to do but actually doing it themselves. Grit is one of the greatest qualities you see in Leaders.

"SO THE QUESTION I HAVE FOR YOU IS, WHY SHOULD ANYONE WANT TO FOLLOW YOU?"

"IT'S A PROCESS NOT AN EVENT!"

1. Motivation

So what is motivation exactly?

When the pain of staying the same becomes greater than the pain of changing. In other words, at some point, it is easier to change than to stay the same. It's easier to take action and feel insecure at the gym than to sit still and experience self-pity on the couch. It's easier to feel awkward while making the sales call than to feel disappointed about your two-digit bank account.

I believe that this is the core of motivation. Every choice has a price, but when we are motivated, it's easier to deal with the inconvenience of action than the pain of staying the same. With motivation, we cross a mental block—usually after weeks of procrastinating and when you have a big upcoming deadline—and it becomes more painful to not do the work than to actually do it.

Now for the important question: What can we do to make it more likely to smash this mental block and feel motivated consistently?

"LEAD THE FIELD BY RAISING THE BAR."

Common Misconceptions About Motivation

What's surprising about motivation is that it often comes after starting a new behavior, not before. We have this common misconception that motivation is a result of watching a motivational YouTube video or reading an inspirational book. But active inspiration can be a far more powerful motivation.

Motivation is the result of action, not the cause of it. Getting started, even in small ways, is a form of inspiration that produces momentum.

Now, remember, I didn't graduate high school but I like to refer to this as the Physics of Production because this is The First Law of habit forming: Objects in motion tend to stay in motion. Once a task has begun, it is easier to continue moving it forward. Energy and Motion together.

How to Get Motivated and Take Action

Many people struggle to find the motivation they need to achieve the goals they want because they are wasting too much time and energy on other parts of the process. If you want to make it easy to find motivation and get started, then it helps to make some early stages of your behavior automatic. They say the road to success leads through the dump, you just don't park there.

Schedule Your Motivation

During a conversation about writing, my friend looked at me and said, "A lot of people never get around to writing because they are always wondering when they are going to write next." You could say the same thing about working out, starting a business, creating art, and building most habits.

If your workout doesn't have a time when it usually occurs, then each day you'll wake up thinking, "I hope I feel motivated to exercise today."

If your business doesn't have a system for marketing, then you'll show up at work crossing your fingers that you'll find a way to get the word out (plus everything else you have to do).

If you don't have a scheduled time when you write every week, then you'll find yourself saying things like, "I just need to find the willpower to do it."

I read an article that said, "If you waste resources trying to decide when or where to work, you'll delay your capacity to do the work."

Setting a schedule for yourself seems simple, but it puts your decision-making on autopilot by giving your goals a time and a place to live. It makes it more likely that you will follow through regardless of how motivated you currently are. And there are plenty of research studies on willpower and the motivation to back it up.

Stop waiting for motivation or inspiration to strike you and set a schedule for your habits. This is the difference between professionals and amateurs. Professionals set a schedule and stick to it.

I learned this when I became an entrepreneur. I was at home with a new business, no boss or time clock. I was the boss and since my business was growing online around the world, I would get distracted being at home watching Sports Center and other sports-related shows that had nothing to do with my business. I read a book by Brian Tracy called "Eat the Frog" and I learned how to prioritize and create a schedule. Benjamin Franklin once said, "If you fail to plan, you are planning to fail."

How to Get Motivated (Even When You Don't Feel Like It)

How do some of the best sports athletes in the world motivate themselves? They don't just set schedules, they create rituals.

The late Kobe Bryant

After 20 seasons with the Los Angeles Lakers and five NBA championships, Kobe Bryant retired from basketball in 2016. But he would still wake up before the sun came up and go to the gym.

There are a few reasons Kobe would maintain such a strict workout routine: "When I first retired, I let myself go a little a bit. ... And then the challenge was, can I get back in shape?" Without an end goal, like an NBA Championship or an MVP award, it's really hard."

To motivate himself, Kobe set specific, measurable goals. "For me, it was, 'OK, I have to aim for something so I said, 'I want to aim for size. I want to aim for bulk. So that's a tangible thing. I'm going to go for that.'"

"We're not on this stage just because of talent or ability. We're up here because of 4 a.m. We're up here because of two-a-days or five-a-days. We're up here because we had a dream and let nothing stand in our way. If anything tried to bring us down, we used it to make us stronger. We were never satisfied, never finished. We will never be retired." The work of people at the top of their industry isn't dependent on motivation or inspiration, they follow a consistent pattern and routine, it's a habit.

Here are some examples of how you can apply ritual and routine to get motivated:

Exercise more consistently: Use the same warm up routine in the gym.

Become more creative: Follow a creative ritual before you start writing or painting or singing.

Start each day stress-free: Create a five-minute morning meditation ritual.

Sleep better: Follow a "power down" routine before bed.

The power of a ritual, or I call it a pre-game routine, is that it provides a mindless way to jumpstart your behavior. It makes starting your habits easier and that means following through consistently easier.

The key to any good ritual is that it removes the need to make a decision: What should I do first? When should I do this? How should I do this? Most people never get moving because they can't decide how to get started. You want starting a behavior to be easy and automatic so you have the strength to finish it when it becomes difficult and challenging.

How to Make Motivation a Habit

There are three simple steps you can take to build better rituals and make motivation a habit.

Step 1: A good pre–game routine starts by being so easy that you can't say no to it.

You shouldn't need motivation to start your pre–game routine. For example, my writing routine starts by getting a glass of water. My workout routine starts by me having my gym bag & pre-workout snacks ready to go. These tasks are so easy, I can't say no to them.

The most important part of any task is starting. If you can't get motivated in the beginning, then you'll find that motivation often comes after starting. That's why your pre–game routine needs to be super easy to start.

Step 2: Your routine should get you moving toward the end goal. A lack of mental motivation is linked to a lack of physical movement. Just imagine your physical state when you're feeling depressed, bored, or unmotivated. You're not moving very much. Maybe you're hanging over like a blob, melting into the couch.

The opposite is also true. If you're physically moving and engaged, then it's more likely that you'll feel mentally engaged and energized. I'll give you an example, it's almost impossible to not feel good, awake, and energized when you're dancing.

While your routine should be as easy as possible to start, it should slowly but surely turn into more and more physical movement. Your mind and your motivation will follow your physical movement. Now, physical movement doesn't have to mean exercise. If your goal is to lose weight, then your routine should bring you closer to the physical act of losing weight.

Step 3: You need to follow the same pattern every single time. The goal of a pre–game routine is to create a series of events that you always perform before doing a specific task. Your pre–game routine tells your mind, "This is what happens before I do ___."

Eventually, this routine becomes so tied to your performance that by simply doing the routine, you get into a mental state that is ready to perform. You don't need to know how to find motivation, you just need to start your routine.

You might realize that your pre-game routine is basically creating a "reminder" for yourself. Your pre-game routine is the trigger that kickstarts your habit, even if you're not motivated to do it.

This is important because when you don't feel motivated, it's often too much work to figure out what you should do next. When you're faced with another decision, you'll decide to just quit. But the pre-game routine solves that problem because you know exactly what to do next. There's no debating or decision making. Lack of motivation doesn't matter. You just follow the pattern. Thats why mindset is very important.

How to Stay Motivated

The best way to stay motivated is to figure out why you started in the first place. You have go back to that feeling of when you started and it motivated you to do it.

I remember when I was on my success journey and there were times where I didn't feel like making that call or going to that next meeting. I would put myself in the right mindset and just see myself where I wanted to be, fulfilling my WHY, and that would give me the willpower to do the things I needed to do. And once I did them, it felt good, was very productive, and got me closer to my goals and dreams.

I learned many years ago that you need to do it first, then you'll feel good. But most people wait to feel good first before doing and then within a blink of an eye, life goes by.

I like to compare this feeling to going to the gym. Most people wait to feel like going to the gym and then they want to go versus going to the gym and then feeling good about it. It's like when I work out at home, I start to think about it then things get in the way. Then by the time you know it, I'll say just do it later... then later becomes tomorrow. Whats worked for me is to join a gym that has classes where you book them (for a fee) and now you're accountable to going with no excuses. And once this becomes a habit it will be a daily routine.

What to Do When Motivation Fades

Eventually, your motivation to perform a task will dip at some point. What happens when motivation fades? Look, I don't claim to have all the answers, but here's what I try to remind myself of when I feel like giving up.

Your Mind is a Suggestion Engine

Think about every thought you have as a suggestion, not an order. Right now, as I'm writing this, my mind is suggesting that I feel tired. It is suggesting that I give up. It is suggesting that I take an easier path.

But if I pause for a moment, I can discover some new suggestions. My mind is also suggesting that I will feel very good about accomplishing this work once it is done. It is suggesting that I will respect what I am building when I stick to the schedule. It is suggesting that I have the ability to finish this task, even when I don't feel like it.

Remember, none of these suggestions are orders. They're options. I have the power to choose which option I follow.

Discomfort Is Temporary

Even when you think about how much you have to do on a daily or weekly basis, nearly any habit you perform is over pretty quick. Your workout will be finished in an hour or two. Your report will be typed by tomorrow morning.

Life is easier now than it has ever been. 300 years ago, if you didn't kill your own food and build your own house, you would die. Today, we whine about our iPhone battery.

You have to maintain perspective. Your life is good and your discomfort is temporary. Step into this moment of discomfort and let it make you stronger.

You Will Never Regret Good Work Once It is Done

Roosevelt said, "Far and away the best prize that life has to offer is the chance to work hard at work worth doing." A lot of times, it seems that we want to work easily at work worth doing. We want our work to be helpful and respected, but we do not want to struggle through our work. We want our stomachs to be flat and our arms to be strong, but we do not want to grind through another workout. We want the final result, but not the failed attempts that come before it. We want the gold, but not the grind. Anyone can want a gold medal. Few people want to train like an Olympian.

And yet, even if I hated doing the hard things, I never found myself feeling worse after the hard work was done. There have been days when it was damn hard to start, but it was always worth finishing. Sometimes, just showing up and having the courage to do the work, even if the result was average, is a victory worth celebrating.

This Is Life

Life is a balance between giving into distraction or overcoming discipline. It's not crazy to say that our lives and who we are is defined in this balance. Life is the result of a hundred thousand daily battles and tiny decisions to either cut it out or give it up.

This moment when you don't feel like doing the work. Don't throw that moment away and not learn from it. This isn't a dress rehearsal. This moment is your life as much as any other moment, spend it in a way that will make you proud.

Motivate the Team

Roosevelt also said, "People don't care unless they see how much YOU care." It's advice that struck a chord with me when I first heard it and I teach it to others to this day.

That's because it gets to the heart of an issue leaders struggle with—how to inspire the people you lead, and keep them inspired.

One of the most important things you can do as a leader is to create purpose. Show your people why you're doing what you do. But what does it take to be that kind of inspirational leader? There's the idea of a "born leader." Are there born leaders or is inspirational leadership a skillset you can learn?

It's a little of both. Studies have shown that great leadership is about 24 percent genetic and 76 percent learned. Natural ability helps, but the most of what goes into making an inspirational leader is about skills and behaviors you can develop.

Knowing that, it makes sense that you can develop the abilities of an effective leader by looking at what other effective leaders do. Here are seven traits and behaviors effective leaders teach others:

1. Authenticity and trustworthiness
2. Positive energy
3. Deep listening
4. Self-awareness and others-awareness
5. Recharging their own emotional batteries regularly
6. Clear vision and core values
7. Centeredness

That's who inspirational leaders are. But that's not where they stop. Effective leaders take those traits and behaviors and funnel them back into their teams. They inspire their teams by:

- Caring as much about people as the business
- Pushing for excellence
- Leading with both "head" and "heart"

- Looking for opportunities to learn from others on the team
- Developing others
- Valuing the input of everyone on the team

Inspirational leaders are identified not only by what they do, but also by what they don't do. Being controlling, negative or fearful will never inspire a team, it'll only kill their motivation. So, as much as leaders need to develop the positive traits of leadership, they need to keep watch and not let negative traits that harm the team creep into their day to day. Negativity, fear of failure, micromanagement or failing to paint a clear picture of your vision, mission and goals are all ways you'll hurt your own effectiveness as a leader. And they'll damage the performance of your team.

"PEOPLE DON'T CARE UNLESS THEY SEE HOW MUCH YOU CARE."

2.
Communication

It's impossible to become a great leader without being a great communicator. I hope you noticed the previous sentence didn't say anything about being a great talker - big difference. This was a hard one for me in my success journey. I remember not wanting to get into conflict with business partners because where I grew up in Los Angeles, that usually ended up in a fist fight. I didn't want to bring that into my business so I avoided communicating completely... but it started to hurt my business. I would let these things drag on too long and kill momentum when all I had to do was communicate and resolve whatever the situation was. So as I started to read books and personally develop and got tired of hurting my business, I knew I had to get good at communicating even as uncomfortable as it was I had to do it if I wanted to be a successful leader.

The key to becoming a skillful communicator is not really taught in school. School teaches us to focus on enunciation, vocabulary, presence, delivery, grammar, syntax and other things like that. In other words, we are taught to focus on ourselves. I don't want to sound like I think that these things are bad, they're important to learn, but it's the smaller parts of communication that they don't teach in the classroom (the parts that focus on others), which leaders need to learn. I want to share a few communication traits, which if you use them consistently, they'll help you achieve better communication results.

Being able to develop a clear awareness is what separates the truly great communicators from those who stumble through interactions with others. If you analyzed the world's greatest leaders, you'll find them all to be amazing communicators. They might talk about their ideas, but they do it in a way which also speaks to your emotions and your dreams. They realize if their message doesn't dig deep inside with the audience then it probably won't be understood and definitely won't be perfected.

I don't think it's any surprise that most leaders spend the majority of their time each day in some type of a social situation. I also don't think it's a shock that a huge number of organizational problems happen because of poor communication. It's this inconsistency that shows us the need for leaders to focus on becoming great communicators. Effective communication is a super important part of professional success at any level of any organization. While developing an understanding of great communication skills is easier than you would think, being able to remember and use those skills when it counts is not always as easy as you might hope for.

These skills and knowledge are only valuable to when they can be practically applied when you need them. The number one thing great communicators have in common is they have a higher sense of awareness depending on the situation and context. The best communicators are great listeners and are sharp in their observations. Great communicators are skilled at reading a person/group by sensing the moods, dynamics, attitudes, values and concerns of those being communicated with. Not only do they read their environment well, but they have the ability to adapt their message to their environment without missing a beat. The message is not about the messenger; it has nothing to do with the messenger; it is 100% about meeting the needs and the expectations of those you're communicating with.

"THE BEST COMMUNICATORS ARE GREAT LISTENERS AND SHARP IN THEIR OBSERVATIONS."

So, how do you know when your skills have gotten to the point that you've become an excellent communicator? You'll know when you have reached the point where your interactions with others consistently use these eleven principles:

1. Don't BS people: Meaning you can smell a phony a mile away. In most cases, people just won't open up to those they don't trust. When people have a sense a leader is worthy of their trust, they will invest time and take risks in ways they never would if their leader had a reputation built upon bad character or lack of integrity. While you can try to demand trust, it usually never works. Trust is created by earning it with the right acting, thinking, and decision-making. Keep in mind that people will forgive many things where trust exists, but will almost never forgive anything where trust wasn't there.

2. Be Real: Stop sending out corporate communications and start having real conversations - dialog not monologue. Here's the thing - the more personal and engaging the conversation is the more effective it will be. There's lots of truth in this statement: "people don't care how much you know until they know how much you care." Classic business theory tells leaders to stay at arms length. I say sure, stay at arms length if you want to remain in the dark and receive only lame versions of the truth. If you don't develop meaningful relationships with people you'll never know what's really on their mind until it's too late to do anything about it.

3. Get to the point: Being specific is better than being unclear 11 times out of 10: Learn to communicate with clarity. Simple and to the point is always better than complicated and confusing. Time has never been more important to people than it is today. It's so important that leaders learn how to cut to the chase and hit the bullet points - but it's also important to expect the same from others. Without understanding the value of being simple and clear, you'll never be given the opportunity to get to the same level as people... they'll tune you out way before you ever get there. Your goal is to weed out the extras, keep it simple, and make your words count.

4. Focus on them not you: The best communicators are not only skilled at learning and gathering information, but they are also experts at transferring ideas, getting everyone on the same page, inspiring action, and spreading the vision. The key is to approach each interaction with a servant's heart. When you truly focus on contributing more than receiving you will have accomplished the goal. Even though this may seem counter-intuitive, by focusing on other people's wants, needs & desires, you'll learn so much more than you ever would by focusing on your own agenda.

5. Have an open mind: I've said before that a closed mind is one of the most expensive things you could ever own. A leader takes their game to a whole new level the minute they willingly seek out those who hold different opinions and opposing positions. But the goal is not convincing them to change their minds but understanding what's on their mind. I'm always amazed at how many people are fearful of opposing views, when what they should be is genuinely curious and interested. Open dialogs with those who confront you, challenge you, stretch you, and develop you. Remember that it's not the opinion that matters, but rather the willingness to discuss it with an open mind and learn.

6. Shut-up and listen: Great leaders know when to dial it up, dial it down, and dial it off (mostly down and off). If you keep talking and not listening you will not have the same result as engaging in meaningful conversation. You have to understand that the greatest form of understanding takes place within a conversation, and not a lecture or a monologue. When you reach that point in your life where the light bulb goes off, and you begin to understand that knowledge is not gained by flapping your lips, but by opening up your ears, you have taken the first step to becoming a skilled communicator.

7. Replace ego with empathy: I have long advised leaders not to let their ego write checks that their talent can't cash. When you communicate openness with empathy & caring and not an over inflated ego, good things begin to happen. Communicators with empathy have this level of authenticity and transparency that those who choose to communicate behind a facade held together by a fragile ego just dont have. Understanding this communication principle is what helps turn anger into respect and doubt into trust.

8. Read between the lines: Take a moment and reflect back on any great leader that comes to mind... you'll find they are skilled at reading between the lines. They have the ability to understand what is not said, witnessed, or heard. Being a leader doesn't give you the license to increase the amount of rhetorical questions and answers. Strong leaders know that you gain so much more by surrendering the floor than by wasting time. In the age of instant communication, everyone is in such a rush to communicate what's on their mind that they fail to realize everything to be gained from the minds of others. Keep your eyes & ears open and your mouth shut and you'll be amazed at how your level of organizational awareness is raised.

9. When you speak, know what you're talking about: Be a master at the subject matter. If you're not the master of what you're talking about, few people will give you the time of day. Most successful people don't have interest in listening to people who can't add value to a situation or topic, but force themselves into a conversation just to hear themselves talk. The "fake it until you make it days" are gone and for most people I know being fast and slick does not equal being credible. You've all heard the saying "it's not what you say, but how you say it that matters," and while there is some truth in that statement, I'm here to tell you that it matters so much what you say. Good communicators focus on both the "what" and "how" parts of communication so they don't fall prey to becoming the smooth talker who leaves people with a bad impression of form over substance.

10. Speak to groups as individuals: Leaders don't always have the luxury of speaking to individuals in an intimate setting. Great communicators can tailor a message so that they can speak to 10 people in a conference room or 10,000 people in an auditorium and have them feel as if they were speaking directly to each one of them as an individual. Knowing how to work a room and establish credibility, trust, and rapport are keys to successful interactions.

11. Adapt - Be prepared to change the message if needed: Another component of communication that people rarely talk about is how to prevent a message from going bad and what to do when it does. It's called being prepared and developing a backup plan. But you have to keep in mind that for successful interactions to happen, your objective has to be aligned with the people you are communicating with. If your expertise, empathy, clarity, etc. don't have the desired effect, you need to be able to make an impact by changing things up on the fly. Use great questions, humor, stories, analogies, relevant data, and when needed, bold statements to help connect and cause the confidence and trust that it takes for people to want to engage. While it is sometimes necessary to "shock and awe" this tactic should be left as a last resort.

Don't assume someone is ready to have a conversation with you just because you're ready to have the conversation with them. Spending time paving the way for a productive conversation is so much better than coming off as the "fake it till you make it" smooth talker. Also, you can't assume anyone knows where you're coming from if you don't tell them. I'm always amazed at how many people assume everyone knows what they want to happen without ever letting people know what their goal is. If you fail to justify your message with knowledge, business logic, reason, empathy etc., you'll find the message will likely fall on deaf ears and need clarification afterward.

Bottom line - The leadership lesson here is whenever you have a message to communicate (either directly, or indirectly through a third party) make sure that the message is true & correct, well reasoned, and backed up by solid logic that is specific, consistent, clear and accurate. Spending a little extra time on the front-end of the message will save you from un-needed aggravation and problems on the back-end. Most importantly, keep in mind that communication is not about you, your opinions, your positions or your circumstances. It's about helping others by meeting their needs, understanding their concerns, and adding value to their world. If you do these things, you'll greatly reduce the number of communications problems you'll experience moving forward.

"EFFECTIVE COMMUNICATION IS A SUPER IMPORTANT PART OF PROFESSIONAL SUCCESS AT ANY LEVEL OF ANY ORGANIZATION."

3. Positivity

Pessimists don't change the world. Throughout history, we see that it's the optimists, the believers, the dreamers, the doers, and the positive leaders who change the world. The good news is, even if you're the biggest pessimist you know, you can learn to change your outlook and that will change your life and make you a much stronger business leader.

When I was starting out in business, it was hard for me to be positive because I was coming from a negative world. I grew up in a tough neighborhood and worked in construction which was a negative environment. I remember talking to people at my job, just normal co-worker stuff, and they would always shoot my ideas down. So when I started my life as a new entrepreneur, I didn't hit the ground running. I had to read books, listen to audios, go to seminars, and just surround myself around the right people. They say you are like the people you hang out with the most. If you hang around people that curse, you'll start to curse. If you hang around people that don't eat the best diet, you'll start to eat like them. It takes someone with a Bulletproof Mindset to be in that environment and remain positive. And as I was learning, I knew that if I wanted to become a better leader I had to become more positive.

Let me give you an example; think about a young boy playing baseball in his front yard. The boy's mom is watching him play from the window. "I'm the greatest hitter in all of baseball!" he says to her. And he throws his ball into the air and takes a swing with his bat.

He misses. "That's strike one!" he says. "Still two more to go, but I won't need them – I'm the best hitter in all of baseball."

He tosses the ball into the air again, and takes an even stronger swing. The ball lands softly next to his feet.

"That's strike two!" he yells. "One more strike to go. Not a problem for the best hitter in all of baseball."

He throws the ball it the air one more time, and again he took an even stronger swing. He swings so hard that he spins around on his heels and falls down onto the grass. The ball lands nearby, untouched.

The boy gets up, dusts off his pants and yells, "Strike three! I'm out!"

His mother says to him, "Aren't you upset you didn't get a hit? After all, you're the greatest hitter in all of baseball."

The boy turns to her and smiles. "No way! Since I struck myself out, I just discovered I'm the greatest pitcher in all of baseball!"

Now THAT is a powerful positive perspective. Finding the good in every circumstance, looking for good instead of searching for the bad.

It's looking at the glass half full, not empty.

Positive leaders are those whose behaviors leans towards the positive extreme, no matter for how long or how difficult the situation. Under this light,
positive leadership has, three super important components:

1. A focus on people's strengths and abilities that remind them about their potential;

2. An emphasis on results that go farther than individual and organizational performance;

3. A field of action that is simple and uses just what any other human can create no matter where they come from.

A recent study estimated that negativity costs the economy $250-300 billion a year and affects the morale, performance, and productivity of teams.

As a business owner, optimism in your company starts with you. If you don't have it, you can't share it. The good news is that pessimism is just a state of mind. It's not permanent. You can change it, and you definitely should.

"OPTIMISM IN YOUR COMPANY STARTS WITH YOU"

Here are some tips to make the life- and business-changing transformation from a negative leader to a positive leader.

Stop complaining and blaming. If you're complaining, you're not leading. Leaders don't complain. They focus on solutions. They identify problems and look to solve them in order to create a better future for all. Positive leaders don't attack people. They attack problems. Be part of the solution not the problem.

Don't focus on where you are; focus on where you're going. Lead your team with optimism and vision. Regardless of the circumstances, keep pointing others toward a positive future.

Look at the Los Angeles Lakers. They lost their best player in franchise history Kobe Bryant, then a month later, the world went into a pandemic. With all that going on, they went into a bubble for months seeing no family just teammates and went on to win the NBA Championship.

Lead with love instead of fear. Fear is draining; love is sustaining. Fear divides; love unites. The key to leading without fear is to provide both love and accountability.

Negative leaders provide a lot of fear and accountability, but no love. If your team knows you love them, they will allow you to challenge them. But love must come first. Former CEO Alan Mulally turned around Ford with both love and accountability. He said you have to "love 'em up," and you have to hold them accountable to the process, principles, and plan. He was able to save Ford and help the economy with a lot of love and a lot of accountability.

Be demanding without being demeaning. Many people think positive leaders are crazy positive who just smile all the time and don't care about results. That couldn't be further from the truth. Positive leaders chase excellence. They believe in a brighter future so they take the necessary actions with excellence to create it.

Positive leaders are demanding but aren't demeaning. They lift others up in order to accomplish their goals, rather than tear them down. They don't talk at you—they walk and run with you.

Connect one-on-one. The greatest leaders connect with those they lead.

People don't care until they see how much you care. Spend time with your leaders connecting with them on something, find common ground and build upon that. Spend time on what they care about not just what you care about. Go where they are!

Create positive change inside-out. Don't let your circumstances and outside events define you. You define your circumstances with your vision, beliefs, and action. Many leaders think they're victims of circumstance. They have an external locus of control. But positive leaders believe they can influence events and outcomes by the way they think and act.

Look at me for example. I became a father at sixteen years old, got kicked out of high school, and was pushed to working in construction… but I didn't let that stop me from being successful. I always heard growing up that it's because I grew up on the "wrong side of the tracks." My mindset kept telling me "Yeah, but I'm not staying there." My current circumstances weren't going to define the rest of my life.

Encourage instead of discourage. Positive leaders are also positive communicators in such a way that they make people around them better and feel encouraged instead of hopeless or discouraged. They also spread positive gossip, listen to and welcome new ideas, and give genuine smiles when they speak. Finally, they are great encouragers who uplift the people around them and instill the belief that success is possible.

Praise in public means recognizing someone in front of their peers, and whisper criticism means coaching them to get better. Both build better people and teams.

There is a power associated with positive leadership. Even if you naturally lean toward a negative outlook, making a few changes can inspire huge changes in your own career success as well as in the success of your team. When you lead with optimism and share positive energy with others, you will transform the negativity that sabotages teams and organizations. Your new positive attitude will finally let you to take on the battle, overcome the negativity, face the adversity, and keep moving forward.

"FINDING THE GOOD IN EVERY CIRCUMSTANCE, LOOKING FOR GOOD INSTEAD OF SEARCHING FOR THE BAD."

"THERE IS A POWER ASSOCIATED WITH POSITIVE LEADERSHIP."

4. Delegation

One of the most difficult transitions for leaders to make is the shift from doing to leading. As a new leader, you can get away with holding on to work. I see a lot of leaders make a big mistake with wanting to do everything themselves because they feel they can do it better or don't trust someone else to do it. The control freak leaders have a hard time with this one.

In the short term you may have the stamina to get up earlier, stay later, and out-work the demands you face. But that will eventually catch up to you, and at that point how you involve others sets the ceiling of your leadership impact. The upper limit of what's possible will only increase with each team member you empower to contribute their best work to your shared goals. But in the same way, your power decreases with every task you unnecessarily hold on to.

According to John C. Maxwell, author of Developing the Leaders Around You, "If you want to do a few small things right, do them yourself. If you want to do great things and make a big impact, learn to delegate."

Delegating for me was not hard at all. I believe in empowering people to get things done faster or even better. I knew I was not good at certain things so I delegated to people that are better. Sometimes I would delegate to junior leaders so they can build their confidence and empower them for the future, even though I knew I could do the job better and faster. It was important for them to grow as a new leader and build their confidence.

That happened to me when I was 23 years old and was headed to a sales meeting. I was new to the technology we were using in my industry and I was going to meet my mentor to learn how to present in future meetings. Now, I think the traffic in Los Angeles at this point is infamous so of course, he got stuck in traffic and was going to be one hour late. He called me and asked if I could get in front of the room and present the information. I immediately had fear set in. I told him "I'm new and don't want to mess up" and all he said was "you got this." So I start the meeting and I'm standing in front of a bunch of people. Everyone was looking at me and remember being so nervous that I had to write bullet points on my hand so I could keep track of what I was going to say. I was so nervous but I had to do it because I was the only one there from our company. As I started to speak, I was trying to look at the bullet points I wrote on my hand and they were smeared because of the sweat from being nervous! I probably looked like a complete idiot but by the time we were done, we had closed 5 deals. To this day, I don't remember anything I said but the deals we closed gave me all the confidence in the world. It immediately taught me that I don't have to wait for anyone. I could go out and do it on my own. It was one of the best things that could have happened to me in business.

That event made me realize that you can delegate and empower people right out the gates. If that hadn't happened to me, who knows what my life would look like.

Put these seven delegation strategies into practice and watch as your organization grows massive.

1. **Let go.** The biggest problem most new bosses and leaders face is that they're not able to let go of their own work. Sometimes they feel so dedicated to completing their own work that they refuse to let other people help.

Other times, they fear that nobody else has the skills or abilities necessary to do the work effectively.

Whatever the case may be, your first priority needs to be to learn to let go. Start small, delegating only the smallest tasks, and slowly work your way up. Get to know your team better and improve the trust among you and your co-workers. Take baby steps and know that eventually you will have to let go of your work if you want your team to be successful.

2. Establish team system. As part of the letting-go process, start developing a team system for tasks. Of course, this system will be a little different depending on your expertise, your industry, and the types of tasks you usually handle, but create at least four categories, according to the degree of effort a task requires and the degree of skill. The highest-skilled category should have tasks that you keep on your own plate, while those in the lower-skilled categories can be assigned to others. The degree of effort should tell you which tasks are more important to delegate--for example, giving someone else responsibility for a high-effort, low-skill task will save you lots of time.

3. Play to your leaders' strengths. As a leader, you'll have to learn the limits of your teammates. You should know each individual's strengths and weaknesses, including his or her current, and potential, range of skills. When you delegate, take a look at your team and assign tasks to whoever has the greatest number of skills made for that task. It seems like an obvious choice, but too many leaders delegate to whoever has the lightest workload or is the most convenient.

It's also important to be consistent. For example, delegating the same type of tasks to the same individual will eventually increase that individual's skill for those tasks.

4. Always include instructions. Even if the task process seems obvious to you, make sure to include instructions with each task you delegate. If you have specific ways for how the assignment will be carried out, include that information. If you have a strict deadline or milestones you need to hit, be clear about them.

Including details and straightforward instructions from the get-go will help you avoid most communication gaps and will allow your tasks to be executed effectively. It's a proactive strategy that both you and your team will appreciate.

5. Don't be afraid to teach new skills. Lacking someone on your team with the ability to execute a certain task on your to-do list doesn't mean the work can't be delegated. Most skills can be learned--some more easily than others--so don't be afraid to teach as a part of the delegation process.

Though the assignment of your first few tasks will take more time than it will save you (since you'll need to train your chosen person), consider it an investment. By transferring those skills, you'll be opening the door to assigning all similar tasks to that person in the future, and in the end it will save you more time than you spent teaching.

6. Inspect what you expect. Once a task is delegated, trust your teammate to execute it on his or her own terms. This will allow the person to tackle the work the way he or she feels is best. However, don't be afraid to sometimes step in and verify that the task is moving along as planned. For example, if you made an assignment a week ago that's due tomorrow, trust that your employee is on top of things, but send a quick verification email to make sure the person hasn't hit a problem that won't allow them to move forward.

Doing that encourages more trust and respect within your team and helps prevent breaks in communication or understanding.

7. Use feedback loops to improve delegation moving forward. Feedback is the most important part of the delegation process, and it works both ways. If your leaders have done well with a task you assigned, let them know by publicly thanking them and offering genuine praise. If they haven't, don't be afraid to give them some constructive criticism.

Remember that it will never be the perfect time to start delegating. You can't wait until you feel that one of your team members gets good at a certain skill. You can't wait until you feel like you wrote the perfect instructions on how to complete a task. And you can't wait until you completely trust someone to do it just like you would... you just have to do it!

"IF YOU WANT TO DO A FEW SMALL THINGS RIGHT, DO THEM YOURSELF. IF YOU WANT TO DO GREAT THINGS AND MAKE A BIG IMPACT, LEARN TO DELEGATE."

5. Creativity

Creative leaders are some of the best leaders you can find. They're always using their creativity to solve problems, bring new ideas and innovation to the team. The idea of using creativity really helped in my business. I was able help innovate systems or offer enhancements to what we already had. The only issue with the creative leader is decision-making. Creative leaders are so creative that they keep creating and don't make any decisions and in the end, no action has been taken. Or let's say you have a system that's proven and works really well but they want to reinvent the wheel with no proven results or they are a brand new leader with no proven success. Listen, I don't like to rain on a new leader's ideas so have them show some success using the current system to create some credibility. Then we can try the new ideas on a small group or project to give it a test run before we let the rest of the company, team, or other leaders know.

Here are five traits the most creative driven leaders all possess.

1. Stirring The Pot

Change is a constant. In the natural world, in politics, in business, the only thing that stays the same is the fact that nothing stays the same. Some people wait until they're thrown into leadership positions by forces around them. But the best leaders—from Joan of Arc to Martin Luther King, Jr. to Steve Jobs—first push themselves into action, then the people around them. They're constantly imagining new possibilities. They instigate change that they envision even when others don't.

The only major difference between these great leaders and the average person is that they're willing to do something rather than let circumstances dictate life for them. That usually means rattling cages and shaking up long-standing beliefs and institutions—which is never easy or well-received. But that's exactly what makes them great. To rise to your true leadership potential, chances are you'll need to rattle a few cages as well, starting with your own.

2. They Take Action Right Away

One of the biggest hurdles for anyone trying to accomplish something is perfectionism—the need to get it exactly right before taking the next step. But the best leaders realize that perfection is impossible, and chasing perfection stands in the way of what's really important: progress. Leadership requires making consistent steps forward, no matter how big. And the quicker the steps, the greater the progress.

Don't buy into the idea that you can take a giant leap if you spend enough time carefully planning it out. By the time you get done planning, other people will run a lap past you twice and already taken that leap you spent months preparing for. Choose instead to "just go" and let the sparks fly. You will make mistakes. But in the process, you'll learn quickly and keep moving and honing your skills and creating new levels of creativity you didn't know you had.

3. They Listen To Intuition

There are things we know to be true and things we feel to be true. Most of us tend to lean on our existing knowledge to solve problems and make decisions. But the best leaders are those who realize that the things they sense—those possibilities like gut feelings and intuition—hold a special value, too. Listening to them is how real breakthroughs happen.

Most of us have problems balancing logic with intuition. But the truth is that those things aren't enemies. In fact, you need to figure out how to get them working together if you're to become a truly creative leader. Intellect without intuition makes for a smart person without impact. Intuition without intellect makes a spontaneous person without direction.

4. They Have Convictions And Stick To Them

"Don't ask what the world needs," the great civil rights leader Howard Thurman once said. "Ask yourself what makes you come alive and then go do that. Because what the world needs is people who have come alive." There's something interesting about a person with conviction, whether or not you agree with everything he or she represents. But conviction is rare, because as we look to solve our need for stability and security, we often make the mistake of looking outside ourselves for direction when we should be looking inside. And over time we can lose sight of who we really are and what's really important to us.

But conviction can be grown from a seed and it starts with you individually. While those who live with great conviction can always inspire you, they don't know your passions and beliefs. Only you can ask yourself, "What makes me come alive?" From there, the gaps between who you are and who you can still be will become clearer. You might find you need something dramatic like a career change, or answering that question that might help you down the path you're already on. The key is to find something that you feel you're meant to do and give yourself to it.

5. They Don't Only Do The Bare Minimum

The ability to come up with new ideas is a defining characteristic of great leaders. They're able to step out of the common vision and imagine new possibilities that set the course for others to follow. Each of us has a huge potential for originality because we're each unique... but activating it can be difficult. Why? Because our lives are full of other demands like our jobs and families and we spend most of our time and energy just trying to keep up.

In order to free your own originality, you need to be willing to stop doing only what's required and expected of you and start doing the things that only you can do, those ideas and projects you keep putting on the shelf until you've got time for them. But the truth is there's never a convenient moment to do them. There's never going to come a time when you'll be 100% certain you'll succeed if you do. Get started on those things today and work on them every day after.

In the end, the real difference between you and the creative leaders who inspire you is action. You have the natural ability to develop all the qualities they possess. The key is to start. Start today, Start now. Don't wait around until life demands something of you—it always will. That's not what leaders do. They take action right away!

CREATIVITY + ACTION = RESULTS

"EFFECTIVE COMMUNICATION IS A SUPER IMPORTANT PART OF PROFESSIONAL SUCCESS"

6.
Trustworthiness

Leaders in today's world have the challenge of earning the trust and commitment of team members if they expect to guide their companies to success in our competitive global environment. Years of trial and error and teaching others has shown me and my leadership team that when leadership behaviors are seen as trustworthy through the viewer's eyes, the trust increases and leaders are more likely to be viewed as ethical masters who honor a higher level of duties.

When I was a junior leader, I use to make mistakes trying to please everyone by committing to attend certain events, meetings, conference calls. The problem was that

I would commit to so many that I wouldn't be able to attend them and then people would call me out and ask why I wasn't there. It wasn't that I didn't want to attend it was that I couldn't be in all those places at the same time. Of course, it was all my fault for over-committing and I saw the results, it affected my business and leadership position with those that were counting on me. I had to grow. The next time I was put in that situation, I would let them know that I might not make it. Even though I didn't want to let them down and it was uncomfortable, I knew I had to do it if I wanted to become a better, trusted leader.

    I would even make mistakes in business deals or transactions. I would say yes to people to get the deal done without reading the fine print or making sure it was the correct amount and man did it cost me. This is one of those processes where I couldn't just go through them, I had to grow through them. I had to become the kind of leader that people could trust. Even though I was just trying to be the good guy and please everyone, I knew I had to stop saying yes to everything.

Since those times, I have helped thousands of leaders around the world overcome this same issue. If you want to be a great leader, trust is important.

"A GOOD NAME IS MORE DESIRABLE THAN GREAT RICHES; TO BE ESTEEMED IS BETTER THAN SILVER OR GOLD."

THE BIBLE

Yes, that's what the Bible said thousands of years ago. It said your "name" or your reputation was one of the most important, most powerful assets you could ever possess.

But if the Biblical wording sounds too old-fashioned for you, try this: "Trust is a must or the relationship will bust." In other words, if you have a "good name," if you are "esteemed" by others, if you are trusted by others, you have one of the most powerful leadership tools you could ever possess. Here are some pointers to becoming more trustworthy.

Do what you say you're going to do.

Nothing creates trust more than keeping your word. Always hold your end of the bargain. If circumstances change, as they usually do, communicate these changes to your team and explain the change in plans and how you'll deliver on your promise. Do it even after the mood you said it in has left you.

You have grace under fire.

No one respects a tyrant. Your colleagues are less likely to trust you if your usual mode of communication involves raising your voice, or humiliating others. When under pressure, buy yourself some time. Take a moment to step back and take a breath before saying something you may regret. Look at text messaging for example. Imagine someone sends you a text that says "Call me." You could take that text out of context because there is no tone of voice to the text. Are they upset? Are they happy? Are they going to yell at you? I always think to myself when I receive a text like that, is this person being demanding or they really just want me to call them back. There are times when people ask me "why am I yelling" on the phone? I'm speaking loudly because I'm driving and I think there's a lot of noise in the background so If I speak louder, they'll probably hear me better. But the other person on the other end might think that I'm yelling at them. Take a step back, then react!

You come to the rescue.

Let's say someone is publicly embarrassed at work, in a meeting for example. Try to find a way to uphold any aspect of what the person is saying and support it. If you can't reinforce any part of it at least say, "What you said just prompted me to consider another idea," before offering an alternative. In other words, help the person save face. I had this happen at an event. One of our speakers was trying to get onto stage and as I was introducing them, they fell. This person was so embarrassed, their face was bright red, and you can hear the crowd of thousands of people start to make noise reacting to what just happened. So I knew I immediately had to do something. I dropped down in a full suit and also fell to them and helped them up, then made a joke out of it and we went on like it never happened. That leader ended up doing an amazing training and no one ever brought it up after the event.

You avoid gossip and cynicism.

Your character gets stained when you gossip. Sarcasm is another characteristic that can create resentment and animosity. People need to be listened to, appreciated, involved and connected. Transparent and direct communication held together with respect, is key. Poison in the river it will kill all the fish and the same thing will happen to your team, organization or business, gossip will kill it. It's like a cancer and you have to be the radiation and destroy it no matter how uncomfortable the situation is or it will keep growing. I always teach people to throw the positives down and around but the negatives up to their leader.

You set realistic targets and offer your help.

Allow enough time for a job to be done well -- the first time. Remain aware of the progress of a project and don't overload others with an unrealistic deadline. If the task is too challenging or time-consuming, ask how you can support them. Arrange for assistance from other team members if needed.

Stop being a control freak.

When you let go of the need to control everything -- you open up the opportunity for your associates to take on more responsibility. Employees are still held accountable and given productive feedback when necessary, but allowing them to take control on occasion kick starts creativity, and helps them to become more resourceful.

You routinely express gratitude.

We all need to hear that our work is valued. Never underestimate the power of "thank you." Remember, what you appreciate, appreciates.

Simply put, you keep your promises. Or as people used to say, "Your word is your bond. You can take it to the bank. It's as good as gold."

So how do YOU stack up on integrity? Do your people trust you to follow through ... to keep your promises? And taking it a step further, do you say what you mean and mean what you say? No double talk? And no fast talk? To be a successful leader, you have to keep your word and do what you say even when you don't feel like it.

"NOTHING CREATES TRUST MORE THAN KEEPING YOUR WORD."

7. Visionary

Think of some of the world's greatest leaders: Martin Luther King, Jr. Nelson Mandela. Oprah. Mother Teresa. Each of them had very different leadership attributes, but they all had one thing in common: a powerful vision not only for their own lives, but for the world. They had an unstoppable belief in themselves and in their dreams.

This type of vision can only come from having a purpose that is so crystal-clear, others see it, too. A purpose that gives your life meaning and leaves you feeling fulfilled. A vision that is so strong you inspire others to join you. Having a clear purpose allows you to not only achieve your goals, but to foster leadership among your team as well.

    When we were launching a company in 2007, we had no guarantee that we would be successful... but we believed we would be. I would do sales presentations talking about the future and how we would own our industry not only here in America but all over the world. I guess you can say we spoke it into existence. We believed in each other because we had been successful before in other business ventures. I could 100% see this team doing it here and that was important because people caught our vision and joined us to build a half billion dollar company in 60 countries. It's so important that you believe in yourself or the idea and just share major vision of where you're going meaning what it will look like when the idea or business is what you ultimately want it to be.

We've all admired such visionary leaders as Steve Jobs, Elon Musk, and Oprah Winfrey. But what, exactly, makes a visionary a visionary? Are these leaders just born that way, or have they developed insights that allow them to see industries in a different way from everyone else?

Being a visionary leader comes from developing specific skills and ways of looking at the world and it's something all of us can learn to do better.

If you want to sharpen your own visionary skills and disrupt your own industry the way Jobs and Musk did, you have to develop these key traits:

Learn to identify trends.

Creating a vision starts with observation. That's why visionary leaders are constantly studying, not only their own companies and industries, but other industries as well.

"Visionary leaders are particularly good at picking up trends and opportunities to disrupt the status quo," Steve Jobs says. "For example, one leader I know does this through rigorous note-taking. He routinely documents his encounters and observations every day, then takes an hour every two weeks to review those notes and look for themes or patterns."

Another approach is to always seek out new experiences. For example, you might try attending at least one event or conference every year on a topic outside of your areas of expertise. "These kinds of intentional actions are practical ways to identify patterns and discover new opportunities," Steve Jobs explains.

Pay close attention to everyday aggravations.

Monitoring trends is only one part of becoming a visionary leader. Another part is close observation of day-to-day business and the ability to use those insights to find new ways of doing things. Let's take a look at an example from IKEA.

IKEA's innovative 'flat-pack' method of selling partially assembled furniture was not originally created in a board room somewhere. Instead, it was a simple observation that several co-workers made after removing the legs from a table to fit it into a car. 'Why should we put the legs on the table in the first place?' they asked.

It was a really good question, and the obvious answer was that they shouldn't, and that was the critical insight that paved the way for IKEA to become the dominant worldwide retailer that it is today.

Look beyond immediate opportunities.

Visionary leaders achieve impact by grabbing opportunities to capitalize on a changing environment. Take one of the original industry disruptors, Walt Disney. His company's success began with its founder's insight not only into the film industry, but also how film's influence would spread to other areas.

While others were focused on creating animated films, Disney famously sketched out a merchandising strategy for his future company on a drawing pad soon after his first feature release. In those early days, Disney could already see how Mickey Mouse and his other characters would expand into an ecosystem that would include theme parks and toys.

In the same way, Jeff Bezos always envisioned that while books were the perfect product to start with, Amazon would one day become a shopping resource for just about everything. So while you're busy taking advantage of the opportunity right in front of you, think about how that opportunity could lead to others to ideas that everyone else hasn't thought of yet.

Don't wait till it's perfect.

Like the first iPhone and iPad, you should plan to improve on your new approach over time. Visionary leaders don't stop with their first attempt. They move through stages of evolution, adapting to accommodate new information and opportunities. Product developers always have dozens of trashed prototypes by the time they have a viable product. In the same way, visionary leaders aren't shy about sharing ideas even when they aren't fully formed, and they don't hold on to an idea when feedback or testing proves that change is necessary.

Get other people to share your vision.

Leaders fail when they assume that a good idea will be obvious to others. You should put as much thought into how to influence other stakeholders as you do into the vision itself.

This was one secret of Steve Jobs' success: He put an enormous amount of work into getting people excited about each new Apple product. His product demos were legendary and prepared down to every single detail. His desire to make sure Apple products were presented to customers in the best possible way even led him to design his own retail stores.

Why will others care? Whose support do you need to make the vision successful? How does your idea benefit them?

Don't make the mistake of just relying on a brilliant idea. "The active support and participation of others can greatly accelerate a vision, while the lack of support can make even the best insights, design, and continuous adaptation irrelevant," he says.

"HAVING A CLEAR PURPOSE ALLOWS YOU TO NOT ONLY ACHIEVE YOUR GOALS, BUT TO FOSTER LEADERSHIP AMONG YOUR TEAM AS WELL."

"VISIONARY LEADERS ACHIEVE IMPACT BY GRABBING OPPORTUNITIES."

8. Time Management

Time management is basically the way that you organize and plan how long you spend on specific activities. It might seem counter-intuitive to dedicate precious time to learning about time management, instead of using it to get on with your work, but the benefits are huge. Spending a little time learning about time-management techniques will have huge benefits now – and throughout your career.

When I started out as a brand new leader in the business world, this was something I needed to learn and implement right away because I was used to being an employee. I had a time I needed to be at work, a time when I needed to get off, and repeat. I was just going through the motions everyday.

But when I became an entrepreneur it was different because I didn't have a boss or someone over my head telling me to do something. I was in full control BUT that can be dangerous as a new entrepreneur because you can get very distracted easily out there just by littlest things. It started happening to me waking up late or not scheduling anything until after that morning. If someone invited me to go golfing, I would reschedule any meeting and go golf. I started putting everything on the back burner but then my business started to get affected by this so I had to change. I needed to develop better time management habits and prioritize the most important things first.

I went an office supply story and bought one of those big calendars for my desk so that I could see it everyday and also see the whole month at a glance. But now we have everything at our fingertips with tablets and phones so there really is no excuse. Then I started to schedule the most important things to do first then second and third and so on. This was a game changer for me and even though it was uncomfortable, it had to be done. They say if you're uncomfortable it's a good thing. It means that you're growing as a person, as a leader, and if you're not growing you're dying.

As a business owner or leader, so many things can keep you from focusing on your main roles — driving sales and pushing your company forward.

That's why guarding your time and managing it well is super important to your success. It's not just about getting it all done — it's also about avoiding getting burnt out and having a sense of accomplishment at the end of the day.

Here's a few time management secrets that will give you refreshing new ways (or reminders) to keep your responsibilities in balance.

Have a short to-do list of your top priorities

What do you want to get done today? What do you want to get done this week? Write down (with a pen and paper) the most important three or five things that come to your mind.

Make sure you break your list down to the task (not project) level. For example, if your project is to prepare for an upcoming show or event, some smaller tasks may be to train your staff on managing your booth space or choosing which marketing materials to bring with you.

Give yourself clear deadlines. Spend about 15-30 minutes to attack this list at the beginning of each day, before unexpected things pop up and steal your time and attention. Physically cross things off your list as you achieve them to give yourself a moment of gratification that will push you onto your next task.

Another option is to make a list at the end of the day of all the things you actually got done. This way you focus on what you accomplished versus what you did not. For some people, this is more motivating. Small daily accomplishments are small victories that turn into big victories. And if you're winning daily this is a great motivator to keep the momentum going.

Use your calendar, and use it wisely

You may have a calendar on paper, on your computer and on your phone. Make one of these – the one that works best for you – the place where you record all of your appointments, your master calendar. Even better, use a calendar that you can access on all your devices to keep you in sync. Thats why I like using my iPhone to input events and tasks because it syncs on all my devices – especially my laptop – so I can see everything at a glance.

Be committed to transferring any appointments you put on paper onto your main calendar. Sometimes, it might make sense to schedule specific times to complete a project or task. Even if you have a knack for keeping a mental record of your schedule, dump the information onto your master calendar and save that brainpower for more important tasks.

Most electronic calendars also let you create several overlapping calendars, like Personal and Work. This is a nice feature to use so that you can make sure you don't double-book yourself, while still having the ability to hide certain calendars and focus on the rest.

In addition to Personal and Work, I use different colors for different types of tasks to identify which one is which. It's so easy to do with technology.

Fewer Problems

Murphy's Law states, "If something can go wrong, it will." And Murphy seems to like to hang around people who have difficulty managing their time. Maybe you know someone who is always late for an engagement because they had to stop for gas, or they missed a meeting because they lost track of time or forgot it altogether. Or they couldn't find their USB drive for the big presentation, leaving other team members to pick up the slack. Stuck in traffic … again. It's often not the circumstance, but a lack of time management that causes these chronic problems. These kind of people are always acting like they have no time and are all over the place. You call them and they're huffing and puffing saying "I need to call you back I'm on the other line." If you're around these type of people it will rub off on you. So get organized and prioritize your time management and this will be a game changer.

Fewer Mistakes

When we feel rushed or behind, it's natural to move through the day's tasks quickly, and rushing usually creates more mistakes. Going back through and fixing errors eats up even more of our time, and it continues the cycle we can find ourselves in. Who hasn't gone to the store without a list, only to realize that they missed a couple of key ingredients after they get home? Or sent an important email with embarrassing typos or promises of an attachment that never got attached?

I say it all the time, I love technology. We have everything at our finger tips! I tell my wife all the time "make a list on your phone or tell Siri to make it for you." I know it's easier said than done but when you write things down or put them in your phone and see them as a reminder, you won't forget something.

This always use to happen to me: I would think of something to get at the store and then I forgot about it, then added something else to the mental list, then I'd end up going to the store and getting the new item but forgetting the old one. It happened so many times that now I make notes in my phone.

Simple stuff like forgetting something at the store is not a big deal but when you start using those same habits and it starts to hurt you or your organization, you'll make a change make it happen.

Successful leaders learn from other peoples mistakes, unsuccessful leaders keep making the same mistakes.

More Respect

Do you know someone who always seems to be prepared? Maybe YOU are that person. People who manage their time wisely not only have the luxury of less stress, they also keep themselves open to more opportunities and respect from those around them. They are typically more dependable, and others count on them to make good on promises. We all want leaders like this in our organization, team, business, etc. There are people like this that have the discipline or are just good at it but one thing I've learned is that if you set the bar high, it will duplicate out to your leadership team because you will expect this out of them and they will see you leading by example. So if you want the respect, you gotta step up your game when is comes to time management.

More Down Time

While it may seem like managing time and staying organized could be a time-sucker all on its own, those who put a good time management system in place find themselves with more free time to do the things they want to do instead of being tied to things they have to do.

Whether you're a person looking to be more successful with day-to-day tasks or a business owner aiming to increase productivity among your team members, time management skills offer a huge number of benefits. Organized individuals are often happier, calmer, more successful (personally and financially), and more productive. If you have a simple system of time management that your team can follow and stay organized, it will free you up and you'll have more time.

Great productivity and time management skills will literally change every aspect of your life!

"IT'S NOT JUST ABOUT GETTING IT ALL DONE – IT'S ALSO ABOUT AVOIDING GETTING BURNT OUT AND HAVING A SENSE OF ACCOMPLISHMENT AT THE END OF THE DAY."

9. Influence

Leadership is misunderstood. People think because someone has a title that they're a leader. Not true, managers and leaders are different. Someone who's in a power position that has the power to fire you is leading based on fear and that's not a true leader. Leaders move and lead people with influence. One of my mentors asked me "If you went to the Red Cross this Saturday to do volunteer work, how many people can you get to show up to volunteer for free with you?" I sat there and thought about who would show up. It's like when I started my first business project and wanted to share it with the people I was close to. I invited them to my house to see it and if they wanted to be a part of it, but not everyone showed up. Who I had the most influence with showed up. So when they asked that question I had an Aha moment and I knew I needed to be more influential if I wanted to be a great leader.

Let's look at Tom Brady who just won his 7th Super Bowl at the age of 43 — on a different team — in his first year there. Because of his influence, he was able to bring some players to join him on this new team and they're the ones who scored all the touchdowns in the Super Bowl. The most important thing Brady brought to his new team was a winning attitude. The entire team bought into the leader and because of that they won the Super Bowl even though they were the underdogs in every game.

"LEADERSHIP IS ABOUT BEING OF SERVICE TO OTHERS"

Start by first reminding yourself that leadership is not dictating, commanding, or imposing. It's being of service to others—to your customers of course but especially to your employees, team, etc.

The Clear Path of Influence

Influence is empowering others to achieve their goals, bringing out the best in people, putting their needs ahead of your own (as a leader), and helping them develop. Think of the multiple ways these things can be done every day.

This is called the servant leadership--one of the highest platforms to launch you toward influencing others. And it's great for your bottom line too, it says a bunch of research.

The behaviors that lead to influence, as written about by thought-leaders like John Maxwell, Stephen Covey, and Simon Sinek, point back to having character. It is who you are, not what you do. It is a choice, not a prescribed process or to-do list.

Are you looking for influence in leading and making decisions? Here's how you do it:

Gain the trust of others.

The foundation for everything related to your leadership has to be built on trust. In his amazing book The Speed Of Trust, Stephen Covey says that "a team with high trust will produce results faster and at lower cost." Normal thinking says that people have to earn trust first, right? But it has been found that in healthy organizations, leaders with a servant mindset are willing to give trust to their followers first, and they give it as a gift even before it's earned. For some people this is difficult if they think their leaders are going to do something bad based off past experiences. But this baggage will end up hurting the organization. It's better to give the trust and then it's given right back and you will build a healthy trustworthy organization.

Let go of your ego.

An unhealthy ego can be a liability on the performance of the organization, just ask the late Kenneth Lay, former CEO of Enron.

I've seen leaders start to believe their own press meaning they get some recognition and start thinking their shit don't stink. They say the pride comes before the fall and I've seen this happen over and over again. Some people have to learn the hard way. Never forget where you come from and never forget where you're going. For me my family keeps me grounded. Growing up in humble beginnings, my parents always taught me to respect people no matter their status or income level. Those values run deep in me and I do my best to implement them in my everyday life, especially when I'm leading people. We all have to walk our walk, not just talk.

You want have a healthy ego, be confident not cocky. Remember that people follow strength not weakness so it's okay to be a strong leader that's confident and knows where they're going. For some people this can be a blindspot so remember that it is also okay to receive constructive criticism. Like I talked about in the Trustworthiness chapter, you need to have an inner circle that gives you feed back. I like to compare it to golfing, you have to have someone watch you or record your swings to see what you're doing wrong and what you need to fix. So having a core group to give you feedback or a coach/mentor is always good.

A leader with a healthy ego is one who has mastered the balance of personal humility with confidence and fierce resolve.

Demonstrate competence.

Sure, a strong character in service to others is crucial. But trust goes out the window if you can't demonstrate knowledge and expertise in your field or industry that will carry the vision forward. Have you ever heard the phrase you can smell a phony a mile away? If people can see that you're full of it or you can't get the job done, they're going to start to lose respect and now the leader is not going to be effective. I had a leader who was a good bullshitter who never wanted to do the actual work, just wanted to tell everyone else what to do. They had a little success and that gave them their credibility so they used that for so long that the people they we're trying to lead never witnessed their actual success. To the growing team, they just heard about it and never actual saw it. And that meant that they were becoming less effective with leading that group, then the business started to be affected and it eventually killed their organization. Don't become that leader. Demonstrate competence and always lead from the front. That includes the ability to communicate that vision, so followers are actively engaged in pursuing it. Competence builds confidence in your people. And their confidence in you, the leader, will ultimately deliver excellence.

Inspire others to find their voice.

In traditional, top-down organizations, bosses at the top of the food chain will lay out a vision, then use power and control to move people to carry out the vision. In today's social economy, leaders will cast a company vision and enroll their followers to express their voice as co-creators and co-contributors to the vision. The fear is pumped out of the room and people are liberated and empowered to collaborate, innovate, and engage. When you do this, it's giving them ownership in the vision and when someone owns a piece of something, they will work harder than the ones that don't because they have skin in the game. Even though they don't own a part of the company, they own part of the vision and that will give them a voice and responsibility to bring their "A game" to work everyday. Remember that most people do the bare minimums so they don't lose their job or leadership position because they don't have any skin in the game. Make them part of the vision to empower them so it duplicates the influence through the organization.

Develop a Community

Companies like Google, Spanx, Tesla, and Apple have distinctive corporate identities that attract great employees. You'll find that these cultures usually center around giving employees ownership over decisions (shared leadership), authenticity (open communication, expression of thoughts, ideas, and perspectives) and the building of community (collaboration, diversity, inclusion).

Community is key because people want to be a part of something. This is why people join gangs or cults, they want to belong, it's human nature. If you build the right community it will attract like-minded people because the wrong type of people can't stand the right type of environment that long.

"DEMONSTRATE COMPETENCE AND ALWAYS LEAD FROM THE FRONT."

"COMMUNITY IS KEY BECAUSE PEOPLE WANT TO BE A PART OF SOMETHING"

10. Decision Making

Effective leaders make decisions quickly. I learned that successful leaders are quick to make decisions and are slow to change and unsuccessful leaders are slow to make decisions and quick to change. Every successful leader I've ever been around are quick to make a decision and go after it and own it.

They may not always be the right decisions in some cases, but the best leaders have the discipline (and the confidence) to make many small and large decisions every day in order to move their businesses forward. So how do they do it without letting fear and doubt stop them? Here's an outline of a few of the key things you need to master that I've learned from effective leaders to help you learn how to make decisions with the same speed and skill.

Surround Yourself with Excellent Advisers

"You never want to be the smartest person in the room." You are as smart as the team you surround yourself with, so make sure you know your weaknesses and hire people to fill those knowledge gaps. Then you have trusted experts to advise you when you have to make decisions that are outside of your comfort zone. Excellent advisers are also great sounding boards. You want peers that will push you to defend your choices so that you make the best ones. Even if its super uncomfortable. Diamonds are made under pressure and the pressure is privilege, it will bring out the best in you.

Confront Your Most Stressful Decisions First

Like I talked about in previous chapters, Procrastination is one of the biggest challenges leaders face. The trouble is that we postpone or avoid what we are most afraid of. Try tackling your most anxiety-inducing problems first so that you get them done and prevent that stress from getting bigger and becoming even more uncomfortable. We also tend to put off decisions that are boring or less exciting than others. Don't let the "boring decisions" hold you back. For example, if you have to make several legal decisions before tax season, don't bump those to the end of your list just so you can focus on user engagement ideas. When you're running a business, the least glamorous challenges are just as important as the most glamorous and exciting ones.

"MIND OVER MATTER!"

In order to be an effective leader who makes positive decisions for your team, you have to be open to constructive criticism. Always ask yourself and your team members how you can improve. Then, strategize for how to execute on the feedback you receive. For example, if you hear that your thought process isn't always readily apparent to your team, try writing a weekly email update outlining the big decisions you made that week, along with a few bullet points as to why you made them and what you hope the outcome will be.

Connect with Your End Goal on a Daily Basis

Leaders make countless decisions on a daily basis, most of which have to be made in total chaos with little information. It's hard to remember your long-term goals when you're faced with dozens of small decisions each day. Check-in with your long-term goals at the end of each day to make sure that you're leading your team in the right direction. As a leader, you need to be able to focus on the details and then rise above trivial issues and see the bigger picture.

Practice Emotional Self-Control

No matter how upset you are, never let your team know that you are anything other than calm and optimistic. As a leader, you hold the key to team morale and company composure. Never show worry, doubt or frustration to your team. Make sure to fine-tune your emotional intelligence so that you create an environment for your team to be successful. A stressful, angry, or anxiety-ridden boss makes for a testy work environment and causes your team to lose faith in your decision-making abilities. Save your frustration, yelling voice, and tears for home. The team demands your best behavior at all times.

I see leaders make this mistake all the time, they wear their emotions on their sleeves and take them everywhere they go, they don't know how to separate your personal and your professional life. I remember asking my team one day if they were excited. They said "yes why?" "Well then you need to tell your face you're excited because it doesn't appear that way." Self control is key: control your emotions especially when it comes to your professional life. It may not be easy in the beginning—it wasn't for me—but you have to grow and get uncomfortable in controlling your mind. That is actually why I wrote the book Bulletproof Mindset because that's what helped me become successful. Mind over matter!

Improve Your Communication Skills

You can be a decision-making genius, but if you can't articulate how your decisions add to the overall goals of your company, you will lose the faith of your team. Being able to effectively communicate your thought process and connect it to the larger company vision is also an essential tool for making decisions. You want to be strategic, rational, and always moving forward. Some leaders limit the time they spend on each decision in order to get to all of their company's needs. To do this, you need to clearly assess a problem, weigh the options, and have a strategy for picking the best one. Let your team be a part of the decision-making process by keeping them in the loop.

Limit Your Options

A study published in the journal Biological Psychology found that people have a harder time making decisions when faced with a greater number of options. The researchers found that strange; people like having a large number of options to choose from but are overwhelmed by them at the same time—which can lead to negative outcomes. Thats why I love In-&-Out Burger. They have three options and even though they have their secret sauce and secret menu, it's still a number 1, 2, or 3. To this day, I've never seen one of their locations that didn't have a packed drive thru.

To help yourself make wise, time-effective decisions, limit your options. Consider three to four possible scenarios, and weigh the pros and cons of each. Any more considerations than that, and you will suffer from too much choice. Remember KISS Keep It Super Simple.

"ALWAYS ASK YOURSELF AND YOUR TEAM MEMBERS HOW YOU CAN IMPROVE."

> "YOU WANT TO BE STRATEGIC, RATIONAL, AND ALWAYS MOVING FORWARD."

11.
What's Next?

I wanted to write a simple book that you could read on a short flight. Sweet, short, and powerful. I wrote this book during a global pandemic and the entire time, I used the past 20 years of growth in leadership to inspire all of my recommendations throughout these past ten chapters. I truly believe that everything rises and falls on leadership and the higher the developed leader, the higher the team can grow.

I would like to leave you with an activity to help you on your leadership journey. On the next few pages, I will have a rating system. I want you to think back to everything you read in these last ten chapters and rate yourself. I'll be asking you two very important questions to determine how you rate yourself.

The first question is "How would you rate yourself?" Be honest but also fill it in with your gut reaction from 1-5. This question is personal to you so you can see where you think you are on a personal level.

The second question is "What do you think your team would rate you?" Think about this, you may rate yourself a FIVE in Trustworthiness but then, when you take a step back and put yourself in the shoes of someone on your team, would they rate you a FIVE? Be honest. Your team could consist of a sales team, peers where you work, your classmates at school, your HOA from your neighborhood, your sports team, or even the family you live with.

Rate yourselves on a scale of 1 through 5. For example, if I were to rate myself a 1 on Influence, that means that I probably couldn't even get my wife to eat at the restaurant that I want to eat at. But if I were to rate myself a 5 in Influence, I could probably start the Church of Angel and everyone would be there on Sunday (just kidding of course!)

After you rate yourself, leave the 90 day section blank. After 90 days, go back and rate yourself again. Did you improve? Did you get worse? I'd love to know! Take a picture and send it over to business@angelolvera.com. Your information doesn't have to be on there, you can send it as privately as you want but I'd love to see the results people are having with this book.

Also, one of the biggest things that helped me become a better leader was my mindset. If you have any doubts about YOUR mindset, I recommend reading my book **Bulletproof Mindset** where I show you the difference of the different mindsets, how they affect your life, and tips on how to improve your mindset and become Bulletproof!

How would you rate yourself?

Motivation

	1	2	3	4	5
Today					
90 Days					

Communication

	1	2	3	4	5
Today					
90 Days					

Positivity

	1	2	3	4	5
Today					
90 Days					

Delegation

	1	2	3	4	5
Today					
90 Days					

Creativity

	1	2	3	4	5
Today					
90 Days					

How would you rate yourself?

Trustworthiness

	1	2	3	4	5
Today					
90 Days					

Visionary

	1	2	3	4	5
Today					
90 Days					

Time Management

	1	2	3	4	5
Today					
90 Days					

Influence

	1	2	3	4	5
Today					
90 Days					

Decision Making

	1	2	3	4	5
Today					
90 Days					

What do you think your team would rate you?

Motivation

	1	2	3	4	5
Today					
90 Days					

Communication

	1	2	3	4	5
Today					
90 Days					

Positivity

	1	2	3	4	5
Today					
90 Days					

Delegation

	1	2	3	4	5
Today					
90 Days					

Creativity

	1	2	3	4	5
Today					
90 Days					

What do you think your team would rate you?

Trustworthiness

	1	2	3	4	5
Today					
90 Days					

Visionary

	1	2	3	4	5
Today					
90 Days					

Time Management

	1	2	3	4	5
Today					
90 Days					

Influence

	1	2	3	4	5
Today					
90 Days					

Decision Making

	1	2	3	4	5
Today					
90 Days					

About the Author

Visit my website at www.angelolvera.com and follow me on my social media to see what I'm up to.

You can reach my team at business@angelolvera.com or fill out the form on my website if you'd like me to speak at one of your events or be a part of our mentorship programs . I can help you and your team/coworkers/family/friends get started on their new careers, new professional journeys, entrepreneurial conquests, just like I did.

Now go and improve on your leadership skills and become the best leader you could possibly be!

www.ingramcontent.com/pod-product-compliance
Lightning Source LLC
LaVergne TN
LVHW051522070426
835507LV00023B/3259